Just a
Small Town
Country Girl

8.11.2011

KAT BUSSELL

ISBN: 978-1-4669-4461-9 (sc)
ISBN: 978-1-4669-4460-2 (e)

Trafford rev. 06/25/2012

 www.trafford.com

North America & international
toll-free: 1 888 232 4444 (USA & Canada)
phone: 250 383 6864 ♦ fax: 812 355 4082

Dedicated To: Gina Anderson

Who would have ever thought
I would some day be a writer
not me, but you know
we all deal with things differently
this is how I deal with things in my life

This is 1 of 2 places I go for writing
as you can see it got over takin' by the flood this year
my inspiration comes from: a word or a phrase
spoken by a friend or even someone I don't know
even from listening to excellent songs
they give me what I need to write
the way that I do

Contents

1) Just A Small Town Country Girl   1

2) Young Love   2

3) The Life We Lead   3

4) You Rock My World Little Boy   4

5) Please Don't Leave Me   5

6) Everything About You   6

7) He's More To Me   7

8) Lay Down Beside Me   8

9) Life   9

10) Getting Into Trouble   10

11) What Can I Do   11

12) Hanging In There   12

13) Hey! I Want You   13

14) You Have A Key To My Heart   14

15) Living In The Past   15

16) Thinkin' Of You   16

17) A Good Nite Kiss   17

18) Our Last Kiss   18

19) A Smile That Would Melt Any Ones Heart   19

20) I So Wish You Knew Me Better   20

21) I Only Want To Love You   21

22) If You Fall   23

23) You're The Inspiration That Holds Me Together   24

24) I've Waited And Waited   25

25) You Gotta Stay Here   26

26) Even In The Dark Of Nite   27

27) Tropical Paradise   28

28) The Roamer   29

29) Just Holding My Hand   30

30) Dreaming Of Leavin'   31

31) Hot & Steaming   32

32) Spending My Time Here   33

33) Walking The Floor Over You   34

34) Listen to Me   35

35) Your Not The Man I Fell In Love With   36

36) I Can't Forget You   37

37) Til We Meet Again   38

38) How Do I Love Thee   39

39) Born Free   40

40) An Amazing Friend   41

41) Good-bye Baby   42

42) When We Were In Love   43

43) Life Isn't A Joke   44

44) Stay Away From Me   45

45) Take Your Love With You   46

46) Don't Get Caught   47

47) Doing The Best I Can   48

48) I Wanna Be Alone   49

49) Had We Never Met   50

50) No You Won't See   51

51) Just Sittin' Here   52

52) Just A Few More Minutes   53

53) Love 'Em An Leave 'Em   54

54) I'm No Angel   55

55) Love You Forever   56

56) Lean On Me   57

57) The Sun Is Coming Up   58

58) Memories {Part 2}   59

59) The Frog & The Prince   60

60) Meant To Be   61

61) Don't Forget To Be Yourself   62

62) Believing   63

63) Waiting My Fate   64

64) Would You Mind   65

65) Just A Simple Girl   66

66) What Are The Things I'm Thankful For   67

67) Lonely   68

68) Leaving The Past Behind Me   69

69) If You Don't Know Me   70

70) Things Happen   71

71) I Want To Hold You Close   72

72) Baby!   73

73) Nothing Ever Stays The Same   74

74) It Doesn't Matter   75

75) Past The Point Of Caring   76

76) Loving You   77

77) Life Is So Complicated   78

78) The Other Side   79

79) How Many Times   80

80) Flying Away   81

81) Walking Thru Life   82

82) Lonesome   83

83) You May Not Miss Me   84

84) God Give Me   85

85) Just A Fool   86

86) Just Don't Give Up   87

87) Find Me A Preacher   88

88) Don't Crush Me   89

89) I Want You   90

90) Cheaters & Cheating   91

91) The Webs Of A Dreamer   93

92) Surprise Me, Baby   94

93) So Easy   95

94) Tangled Up In You   97

95) Enjoying My Time   98

96) He Came To See Me   99

97) You Say It Best   100

98) Tropical Paradise #2   101

99) What's Your Dream   102

100) To Catch A Falling Star   103

101) Elizabeth   104

102) Heaven   105

103) I'm Letting Go   106

104) The Hospital Kitten   107

105) My Life   108

106) Miles Between Us   109

107) Putting My Heart On The Line   110

108) Listen With Your Heart   111

109) You Know It's Not   112

110) Walking Away   113

111) Can I Keep You   114

112) To All My Online Sisters   115

113) The Most Amazing Night   116

114) Lonely Is Real   117

115) The Facts Of Life   118

116) You Gotta Love Me, Forever   119

117) Just A Drop In The Bucket   120

118) Angels   121

119) I Have Better Things   122

120) A Great Friend   123

121) Encouragement   124

122) Nothing Is Out Of Reach   125

123) Fight Harder   126

124) I Must Admit I Never Thought Until Now   127

125) With Every Trial   128

126) No More   129

127) Who Is My Destiny?   130

128) Love Hurts   131

129) Inside   132

130) Marked For Love   133

131) Miles Of Trouble   134

132) The Best Of My Love   135

133) Love At Last   136

134) The Broken Heart   137

135) Lost Hope   138

136) My Idea Of A Perfect Man   139

137) No Heart Of Stone   140

138) Bottled Up Emotions   141

139) No End To My Struggles   142

140) Angels Lookin' Over You!   143

141) One Day Soon   144

142) Two Ships Passing In The Night   145

143) There Is A Fire Burning In My Heart For You   146

144) A Long Lost Love   147

145) My Singing Heart   148

146) The Woods   149

147) One Moment   150

148) Feelings   151

149) Stop Living In The Past   152

150) A True Dreamer   153

Just A Small Town Country Girl

Just a small town country girl
born and raised in the country
doesn't know no other life
went to the city and felt outta place
run back to the country life
cause it suited her world
it's all she knew and loved
livin' in the peace and quiet
doing what she wants, when she wants
just a small town country girl
born and raised in the country
doesn't know no other life

Young Love

Young love isn't it great
you really don't understand
what love really is at that age
but crushes come and go with time
some you wish would last forever
but a few years if your lucky
some have truly found true love
and it has lasted them forever
til death do we part
young love isn't it great
you really don't understand
what love really is at that age
but crushes come and go with time
letting go of your true love
once they are gone is hard for some
cause they had what it takes
to keep their love alive
they never strayed from their soul-mate
young love isn't it great
you really don't understand
what love really is at that age
but crushes come and go with time
I haven't found love yet
I'm hoping that one day it will find me
til then I will wait patiently
for it to find me some day

written: Dec. 13, 2011
at 8:55 pm

Inspired by: Vickie Minich Manners
& Shaun Cassidy

The Life We Lead

We all lead very different lives
some are gifted and wise
everyone has very different vibes
we need to be lifted and rise

there are those who are teachers
some love to sell things
then you have your preachers
and those who love to build things

there are those who can fly planes
those who drives trains
some men like to work with cranes
there are the Indians who ride the plains

but we all have our choices in life
you have to do what makes you happy
stand up and voice your thoughts
you have the right to be heard
only you can choose your right to happiness

written: Nov. 8, 2002

You Rock My World Little Boy

You rock my world little boy
you make me feel like a whole person again
something I haven't felt in a long, long time
I closed off my heart to pain some time back
closing everyone and everything from it
I felt I'd had enough pain
to last three lifetimes and then some
life hasn't been easy on me
things I thought were looking up for me
but I was wrong yet again
will I ever find happiness
I don't know right now what happiness is
because I've never been truly happy
what I had first I was happy
had the man I loved
we were expecting out first child
things couldn't have been any better
in my world
unless I'd died and gone to Heaven
you rock my world little boy

Please Don't Leave Me

Please don't leave me
we haven't even givin' love a chance
it could work out if we'd let it
don't give up on us
give it a little more time
what do you have to lose
it won't cost you anything
just a piece of your heart
that's all I'm asking for
we can take it one day at a time
to see what might happen between us

written: Jul. 22, 2011

Everything About You

Everything about you
makes me wanna cry with joy
as the tears run down her face
he slowly runs his finger over
every tear that runs from her eyes
wantin' to see her beautiful face
that he had fallin' in love with
as he looks at her his heart swells with pride
although he was excited to finally find her
he knew deep inside his heart
he didn't want to lose her
she had become his world
in such a short time
he had fallin' for the beautiful woman
who would now be his wife
til the end of time
I love you, honey

written: Jul. 22, 2011

He's More To Me

He's more to me
than what I wanted in a man
he's full of compassion & love
he cares about how I am
supportive in everything I do
loves me unconditionally
he's more to me
than what I wanted in a man
he will be kind & curtious
open a door for me
make sure I have everything I need
if not go get what I need
he's more to me
than what I wanted in a man
he will be honest & understanding
call me when I'm home sick
just to make sure I'm ok
take good care of me
when I need it
he's more to me
than what I wanted in a man
he's more to me
than what I wanted in a man
he's more to me
than what I wanted in a man

written:Jul. 22, 2011

Lay Down Beside Me

Lay down beside me, honey
hold me ever so close to you
as if you're afraid that I might leave you
love me tonite like you never have
kiss me as if you haven't seen me in a while
hug me as if your arms are on fire
I want to feel treasured & loved tonite
as I'd want you to feel like

written: Jul. 22, 2011

Life

Life is not like a fairy tale
it has it's ups & down's
you gotta go with the flow
and know the difference
between right & wrong

life is like a two way street
you have to give & take
in order to get – you gotta give
to receive – you gotta be honest & sincere

sometimes life can stink
but life can be good to
it all revolves on how you treat others
treat others as you'd
want them to treat you
and everything else will fall in to place

written: Nov. 4, 2002

Getting Into Trouble

I just can't seem to do anything right
no matter how hard I try, I always fail
it's never enough for people
they want more & more from you
I'm tired of trying to please everyone
I am in misery over all this
trouble seems to follow me everywhere I go
sometimes I wish it would all go away
but that is only wishful thinkin' on my part
why can't people just leave me alone
and let me live my life the way I want to
they have no business telling me what to do
or how to do it, I'm a big girl
I am responsible for my own life
not anyone else so go away and leave me be

written: Nov. 6, 2002

What Can I Do

What can I do
to help you understand
how I feel about you
actions speak louder than words
so maybe you will understand
won't you give me that chance
to show you just what
you mean to me
Come on baby give me the chance
to prove my love for you
let me love you baby
you just might enjoy it
you never know do you
what can I do
to help you understand
how I feel about you
what can I do
to help you understand
how I feel about you

written: Jul. 24, 2011

Hanging In There

Hanging in there
is what I do best
always waiting to see
what is around the corner
even though at times
it scares me a little
life & love are so uncertain
these days
you never know whats waiting for you
just around the corner
hanging in there
is what I do best
waiting to hear from you
waiting to see your face
always waiting to see
what is around the corner

written: Jul. 24, 2011

Hey! I Want You

Hey! I want you
I need your love
I need a special kind of attention
one that deserves the best
that you can offer her
a love that lifts you up
a love that builds bridges
between your heart and hers
that binds you to her
and only her
as her heart builds bridges to your heart
Hey! I want you
I need your love
to survive in this lonely world

written: Jul. 26, 2011

You Have A Key To My Heart

You have a key to my heart
you can't give it away
nor can you give it back to me
it's non-returnable
only you can use it
when you need me
I'll be there for you
waiting to support you
loving you forever & for always
you have a key to my heart
you can't give it away
nor can you give it back to me
it's non-returnable

written: Jul. 28, 2011

Living In The Past

Living in the past
won't change any of the
mistakes we have made
it only causes you more pain
to dwell on the past
and the huge mistakes we made
to remember everything you treasured
during that time in your life
for years I did this
the only thing it got me
was more pain to deal with
you now have a future to look forward to
and who you want to share that with
don't throw your future away
living in the past

written: Jul. 30, 2011

wagon wheel with pink roses
goes with this poem

15

Thinkin' Of You

Thinkin' of you nite and day
wondering how you are today
and if you miss me at all
thinkin' of you now and again
hoping everything is ok with you
wondering when I'll see you again
or if you wanna see me again
thinkin' of you nite and day
wondering how you are today
and if you miss me at all

written: Jul. 30, 2011

A Good Nite Kiss

A good nite kiss
that leaves you feelin' young again
the kiss that tells you, how I feel about you
the kiss that rocks your world
and sets your heart on fire
your pulse strong and pounding
the kiss that turns you inside & out

written: Aug. 4, 2011

Our Last Kiss

This is our last kiss, forever
never to be kissed by each other again
I hope that you will always remember what you gave up
when you realize you've made a mistake
please don't think that I will take you back
you had me and ordered me out of your life
even thou I didn't want to leave you
I knew I had to let you go and move on
move on with my life without you in it
love is a wonderful thing, granted to very few people
love is a two way street, you gotta give love
in order to receive love back two-fold
love is unconditional for two people
you either love someone or you don't
but don't lead them on if you don't love them
it is wrong to treat someone like crap
and make them feel worthless in life
I'm sure you wouldn't want to be treated that way

A Smile That Would Melt Any Ones Heart

A smile that would melt any ones heart
keep on smiling it makes my day, honey
it makes me want to smile as well
what a great feeling that is, honey
to know that life is still wonderful to this day
and that you make it better, day by day,
by just your sweet smile, your kind words
your warm gentle heart, that's what I love about you
a smile that would melt any ones heart
keep on smiling it makes my day, honey
it makes me want to smile as well
smiling has been something that I didn't do much of
in the past due to being unhappy and sad

Kat Bussell

I So Wish You Knew Me Better

I so wish you knew me better
you would know that I'd never
do anything to hurt you my friend
I would do anything and everything
to make your life better because I care
I will always be here when you need
someone to hold you, to listen to you
to give you the comfort of a friend in need
I will always care about you no matter
what comes your way or my way
I so wish you knew me better
you would know that I'd never
do anything to hurt you my friend

written: Sept. 6, 2011

I Only Want To Love You

I only want to love you
I want the chance to show you
how much I care about you
won't you at least give me a chance
you will not be sorry, honey
I love you so very much
look into my eyes and tell me what you see
tell me that you see what I'm saying is true
that I love you with every fiber of my being
that I want to make you happy for the rest of your life
I only want to love you
I want the chance to show you
how much I care about you
won't you at least give me that chance
I love you so very much
what could be better than what I am offering you
do you really want to spend your life alone
to have no one to care about you
no one to take care of you when you're sick
do you really want to shut me and the world out
I only want to love you
I want the chance to show you
how much I care about you
won't you at least give me that chance

Kat Bussell

I love you so very much
think of all the things we could do together
do you really want to miss out on all those things
or is it just me you don't want to be with
tell me the truth I deserve that much from you
I want to spend the rest of my life with you
wouldn't you like to spend the rest of your life
with someone who loves you for who you are
someone to laugh with, to watch a scary movie with
then at the end of everyday you can tell the one you love
just how much you love them and that you're glad
they came into your life just when you needed them most

written Sept. 7, 2011 at 2:09 am

If You Fall

If you fall
I will be there to catch you
To keep you from getting hurt
it's just something you do
out of the love of your heart
I don't wanna see you get hurt
I will be waiting for you to need me
I will never be far behind you
keeping a close eye on you

You're The Inspiration That Holds Me Together

You're the inspiration that holds me together
I need you in my life
your love is what thrills me to the bone
your gentle nature to live life
to make every day count to the fullest
to enjoy the true meaning of happiness
to love unconditionally no matter what
you're the inspiration that holds me together
I need you in my life

I've Waited And Waited

I've waited and waited
for 17 years I've waited
had my heart ripped out so many times
I just wanted to give up
but I held on for dear life
hoping that the star I was
wishing on would grant me my wish
those 17 years have come and gone
memories that should have been mine are gone
I have no way to get them back now
and still I wait to be a part of your life
that was denied me all those years ago
I go back in for open-heart surgery
will I be denied the time with my kids
I have always loved you!!!

written: Sept. 22, 2011

You Gotta Stay Here

You gotta stay here
you can't go with me
even though I know you
wanna go with me
and I'd love to take you
with me, but I can't
I hate to leave you behind
it breaks my heart to leave
you behind honey
you will always be the one
true love, of my life

written: Sept. 21, 2011

Even In The Dark Of Nite

Even in the dark of nite
things are not what they seem to be
darkness is really lite with a huge shade
covering over it not everyone can see this
take off your blinders
take a look at everything around you
what does all this mean to you

written: Aug. 29, 2011

Tropical Paradise

Let your mind go let it
travel to a tropical paradise
where everything is in full bloom
the sun is out and bright
the weather is warm on your face
what a tropical paradise
the only thing is, it is in my mind
can't have a tropical paradise
while your in the hospital
suffering from A fib
so my mind has takin' flight
escaping to that unknown destination
where no one is just you and nature
the perfect sandy beaches
the bright stars against the dark blue sky
Oh what a sight!!!

written: Aug. 28, 2011

The Roamer

Roaming the halls of second floor constantly
watching everything I pass by never
missing a thing that is going on
taking each day, one day at a time
one minute by a minute, one second by a second
hoping that the next day will be better than
the last and I will be able to leave here
and go home where I can be myself again
and not a sick patient waiting to be told
you can go home girl get out of here
I will miss roaming the halls of the second floor
but I will miss the girls who took
such great care of me while I was there
thanks for caring enough to make
me comfortable while I was there with you
you are a treasure to your patients
love and respect go a long way in my book
and I can honestly say, "Thanks"

written: Aug. 29, 2011

Just Holding My Hand

Your just holding my hand
and let me say, "How wonderful that feels"
I've missed that for such a long time
it's nice to have someone who will hold it
or to just put your arm around my neck
and walk beside me like it's something
we have always done together, forever
time may have separated us way back when
but time has brought us back together, again
it is wonderful to see you again and
spend time with you that we lost way back when
when we were young and didn't really
understand how the world worked

written: Sept. 30, 2011

Dreaming Of Leavin'

Dreaming of leavin' this place
movin' to the next stage of my life
the stage of my life that thrills you
beyond anything you could imagine
happier than you could ever thought possible
in the world we live in today
exhausted of living a life of:
pain, abuse and over bearing people
who thinks they know what is best for you
now looking forward to each new day
a day filled with fun & excitement
dreaming of leavin' this place
movin' to the next stage of my life

written: Sept. 24, 2011

Hot & Steaming

He was so hot & steaming
you could see it raising
from his body as he worked hard
his skin steaming from sweat
from baking in the sun
you just want to cover him
to stop the baking process
in the golden sunlight
just to put my arms around him
and hold him close to my cool skin
to pay tribute to his steaming hot body
oh oh baby
holding you close to
my heart and cool skin

written: Sept.25, 2011

Spending My Time Here

Spending my time here
laying in this bed, recovering
waiting to go home so bad
to the things & friends
that I missed so much
oh how I miss
the comforts of home
the conversations with my friends
oh how I miss these things
you don't realize how much you miss
when those things aren't in your life
at the present time
spending my time here
laying in this bed, recovering
waiting to go home so bad
to do the things I missed doing
to love the things that I cherish in life
my friends & my family
oh how I miss those things right now
wishing I could be at home
doing the things I miss doing

written: Sept. 25, 2011

Walking The Floor Over You

Walking the floor over you
walking the distance between us
trying to get nearer to you
but you seem to get further away
with every step I take towards you
why can't I get close to you
I feel as if your backing away from me
so that I won't get close to you
do you not want me
is that why you seem so far away
the distance is short between us
or so it seems
walking the floor over you
walking the distance between us
maybe your not their at all
maybe I'm wrong and just seeing things
you could be a figment of my imagination
but I doubt that you look so real to me
I wanna be close to you forever
to be all the things you need me to be
not just as a lover but also as a friend
who you can talk too, someone you can laugh with
someone you can share your dreams with
someone you can cry with in a time of sorrow
over a lost love one who had to leave
walking the floor over you
walking the distance between us

written: Sept. 25, 2011

Listen to Me

Listen to me carefully
if you think I'll stay and take
your abuse watch this, little boy
I'm walkin' out of your life
I don't want to be with you anymore
you didn't treat me right, little boy
you didn't love me enough, little boy
to make our relationship work
I'm outta here, leavin' you behind
I'm movin' on with my life
so you can get over yourself
and for once in your life
think about someone else first
instead of what you want & need
listen to me carefully
if you think I'll stay and take
your abuse watch this, little boy
I'm walking out of your life

written: Aug. 2, 2011

Your Not The Man I Fell In Love With

Your not the man I fell in love
with anymore, honey
you have changed so much on me
that I don't even know who you are anymore
I'm not the center of your world
you've ignored me time & time again
left me feeling lonely & confused so many times
as to what I want in life now, I don't know
I'm somewhat scared of being alone now
knowing this do you feel big & important now
that you have made a woman lonely & confused
afraid of opening that new door, called life
the door were I step thru and leave you in the past
and move on without you as a part of my life
to be beside me forever and ever
your not the man I fell in love
with anymore, honey
you have changed so much on me

written: Aug. 2, 2011

I Can't Forget You

I can't forget you
no matter how hard I try
you're right their in my mind
reminding me of what I had & lost
always wishing for what I'll never have
that one person to love me
for who I am {me}
I'm just me now & forever
I don't pretend to be someone who I'm not
don't care about fancy house or cars
don't need a lot of money to be happy
all I really need is you in my life
to love me, hold me, kiss me
I can't forget you
no matter how hard I try
you're right their in my mind
reminding me of what I had & lost
Our life together has come & gone
you had me, had my love, and my heart
but you decided it was time to end
what we shared together for a short time
it's over and done you & me
as time passes I hardly remember you
and what you did to me

written: Aug. 3, 2011

Til We Meet Again

Til we meet again
you will never be far from my heart
or far from my mind
there won't be a day that goes by
that your not on my mind
wishing the best for you
and hoping that life is treating you well
til we meet again
you will never be far from my heart or far from my mind
hoping & praying that all your dreams come true
that you would be encouraged to help others
who needs help, but is afraid to ask for it
afraid of being rejected yet again
don't push to find out why they won't ask for help
it will only scare them away
the problems will continue to go on and on for them
with no hope of it ever ending for them
just be the friend they need right now
that means more to someone than anything else would
til we meet again
you will never be far from my heart
or far from my mind

written: Sept. 16, 2011

How Do I Love Thee

How do I love thee, my love
now honey, let me count the ways
I love the way you smile at me
with that look of innocence on your face
but I can see that mind of yours working
on what you are really thinkin'
your such a bad boy, honey
I so love that about you don't ever change
the way that you care about me
when I'm not feeling good
your always wanting to know if I'm okay
always making sure that I have what I need
and when I need it, thank you, honey
if I'm down some days and just can't smile
you'll say something to cheer me up
or make me laugh at something cute
I love all these things about you, honey
I don't know how I got so lucky to have you
to have you in my life just when I needed you

Kat Bussell

Born Free

Born free, living the way I want to
I don't need any advice from you
people who think they know more about
me & my family than I do
and knows what needs to be done
in my life & the lives of my family
I know whats best for my family & me
go live your own life and leave
me alone to do whats best for family
I don't tell you what to do with your family do I
what gives you the right to tell me what to do
with my family
born free, living life the way I want to
I don't need any advice from you

written: Sept. 25, 2011

An Amazing Friend

There is an amazing friend
waiting to make your day special
you are foremost on their mind
I want you to know how special you are to me
you mean the world to me, my friend
no one could ever take your place
because they already have there space
buried deep inside my heart
you all have that special place in my heart
no matter what happens in life
we will always be together in spirit
closer than any family ever realized

written: Aug. 30, 2011

Good-bye Baby

Good-bye baby, good-bye baby
you wanted me gone from your life
I left even thou it hurt me dearly
I'll never forget you or the way you treated me
you were cold and mean to me
so not worth being treated in such a fashion
I wish you well in your life
but if you ever run across a woman who takes
you for everything you got, you deserve it
for the way you treated me while we were together
I hope she breaks your heart wide open
like you broke my heart in two
good-bye baby, good-bye baby
you wanted me gone from your life
I left even thou it hurt me dearly

written: Sept. 2, 2011

When We Were In Love

When we were in love
your universe was next to mine
loving you was all we wanted
from each other
living day by day on love
filling the void in our lives with love
I gave you my heart fully
dreaming of walking that long highway
with you called life's highway
when we were in love
your universe was next to mine
but things had changed between us
you no longer loved me
and now I walk that long highway alone
unwanted & unloved
granted it hurt more than I'd like to admit
but honestly I'd rather be alone
than with someone who refuses to love me
when we were in love
your universe was next to mine

written: Sept. 17, 2011

Life Isn't A Joke

Life isn't a joke
it takes a lot of work to survive
it takes a heart of stone
it takes courage to walk
thru the spaces of time
life is stimulating sometimes
if your with the right person
your soul-mate for life
it takes a lot of respect for others
to survive each new day
life isn't a joke
it takes a lot of work to survive
no matter what comes your way
you must learn to cope with what hits you
even thou your not sure you can do it
you can do anything you want
if you want it bad enough
it takes a lot of compassion for others
to survive each new day
life is not a joke
it takes a lot of work to survive

written: Sept. 17, 2011

Stay Away From Me

Stay away from me
leave me alone
I don't want to be around you
I loved you
and you threw it all away
all because you wanted someone else
you got what you wanted
me gone from your life
you can deal with the after effects
I don't have time to deal with you
I have a life to live
and I plan to live it in peace & harmony
as it should have been from the beginning
I made a mistake with you
thinkin' that you could love me
I won't make that mistake again
nor do I want any part of you
stay away from me
leave me alone
I don't want to be around you

written: Apr. 19, 2011

Kat Bussell

Take Your Love With You

Take your love with you
along with your heart
I don't want either
I don't need you around
I can make it on my own
I once upon a time
needed a man in my life
but not anymore
take your money with you
I don't want or need it
I can survive on my own
I can survive without you
can you hear me, listen carefully
I don't need you anymore

written: Apr. 20, 2011

Don't Get Caught

Don't get caught
with your heart on your sleeve
you just might fall in love
without even realizing you
have fallen hard for someone
even though it was not what you wanted
sometimes things in life just happen
beyond our control
but if we could control it
it takes the mystery out of life
and what fun would that be
if everything was controlled by you
there would be no more fun in life
as we know it, what a mistake
you'd be bored with your life
as we know it to be at times
don't get caught
with your heart on your sleeve
you just might fall in love

written: Apr. 20, 2011

Doing The Best I Can

I'm doing the best I can
I'm just one person
in a world over a million people
I'm not superman
I can only handle so much
til I need help from others
I'll do what I can, when I can
please know I'm trying
that's more than some do in life

written: Apr. 23, 2011

I Wanna Be Alone

I wanna be alone
go away and leave me alone
I need time to think
as to what I want out of life
as to what I need from you
if I even want to be around you
can't you give me some time
to think about everything
that has happened between us
I need a little space from you
please go away
I wanna be alone
go away and leave me alone
I need time to think

written: Apr. 23, 2011

Had We Never Met

Had we never met
you wouldn't know me today
nor would I know you today
you wouldn't care about me
nor would I care about you
some things are just meant to be
you can't fight things you don't like
nor can you win against fate
fate always wins in the end
no matter if you like it or not
life has changed for me
you came into my life
you made me come to life again
I didn't think that was ever possible
when I wanted to cry my heart out
I knew I shouldn't care, but I do
the only thing is
will you rip my heart out
like all the rest of the men
who have come & gone in my life

written: Sept. 7, 2011

No You Won't See

I've been waiting for you
cried many times for you
but I won't show you my tears
that is something I'll keep private
no you won't see
my tears will weep from my heart
instead of from my eyes
the pain is felt in my heart
not from my eyes that
might mist over a time or two
no you won't see
the pain you have caused me
not really sure I deserved this
but then life isn't easy either
you can give and give
til you think there is nothing left
to give someone
are you willing to give it up
are you willing to let go
no you won't see
the pain you have caused me

written: Jun. 6, 2011

Just Sittin' Here

Just sittin' here staring
out into the water
not really seeing anything
just wishin' I wasn't in
so much pain of being lonely
how do I describe the pain I feel
oh how I wish I could explain it
but words would not do the pain
justice of how I feel
life moves on around me
but I can't get excited about it
the sun is just starting to set
for the night and not even
that thrills me at all
I love sunsets with
all the beautiful colors
streaming across the beautiful
blue skies with the small white clouds
that look like snow covered mountains
just sittin' here staring
out into the water
not really seeing anything

written: Oct. 9, 2011

Just A Few More Minutes

Just a few more minutes
til I'll see you once more
just stopping in, honey
to tell you, "I love you"
and your on my mind
while we are apart
the day will come, honey
when we are together
til the end of time
and that everyday with you
is brighter than yesterday
because your the lite, the way for me
and I have you to come home too
just a few more minutes
til I'll see you once more

written: Oct. 8. 2011

Kat Bussell

Love 'Em An Leave 'Em

Love 'em and leave 'em
men do it all the time
it's time to turn the table
come on women we can do it
love 'em and leave 'em
just like they do us
let's see how they like it
whisper sweet nothings in their ears
that we can't live without them
that their world revolves around ours
then turn around and walk away
as if it had meant nothing to us
don't return their phone calls
don't wish them a great day
just ignore them like they do us
love 'em and leave 'em
men do it all the time
it's time they get a taste
of their own medicine
stomp on their heart
as if it meant nothing to us
it's way past time for us
to teach them a lesson in love
women have feelings
we are not play toys
love 'em and leave 'em
men do it all the time

written: Oct. 12, 2011

I'm No Angel

I'm no angel
I'm not perfect
I've got my faults
everyone does
nobody is perfect
except for God
everyone does things
differently
there's nothing wrong
with being unique
it's what makes you
who you are as a person
life is what we make of it
I'm no angel

written Jul. 30, 2006

Love You Forever

I will love you forever
I promise you my love
forever and ever until eternity
I want to walk with you thru life
down that long highway
I promise to be faithful to you
and hope you will be faithful to me
I want honesty, honey
I promise to be honest with you
I will love you forever
I promise you my love
forever and ever until eternity
I want to know I can trust you
and show you that you can trust me
with a love so pure
honey, I love you so
I wanna grow old with you
I love you so

written: Oct. 16, 2011

Lean On Me

Lean on me
I'll hold you up, honey
when you need me
I'll be there for you
always and forever
lean on me
I'll hold you up, honey
when you need me
love you always
wanna be with you
day after day
lean on me
I'll hold you up, honey
when you need me
you can count on me being there
when you need me the most
I will never turn away
nor will I ever leave you

written: Oct. 16, 2011

Kat Bussell

The Sun Is Coming Up

The sun is coming up
it's so beautiful
the yellows, oranges, pinks & blues
are so breathe takin'
oh what a wonderful sight
I love watching the sun come up
so wish I had someone to watch it with
I so miss having that
in my life at this time
the leaves on the trees
are changing colors right now
they look so beautiful when the sun
comes up behind them
the colors seem more brighter
against the skyline
it is so breathe takin'
it's something that no one should miss
out on in their life
life is so short for all of us
it's a shame to miss out on such beauty
this is what memories are made of
memories last forever in your heart & mind
they will always be their for you
to remember the good times in your life
we all have good & bad memories
they make us who we are
even if we know it or not

written: Oct. 17, 2011
at: 7:35 am

Memories {Part 2}

*The great thing about memories
they shape who we are
what we inspire to be in life
and they are always with you
some old memories are good
but it is important to
make new memories as well
memories you can share with
family & friends
the stories behind each of those memories
all with a meaning worth sharing
all deserve to be shared with your
love ones & your special friends*

written: Oct. 17, 2011

*put pic of Wellington–Napoleon R–9
school pic on this poem*

The Frog & The Prince

The frog & the prince
the men in my life have been
frogs who turned into a nice guy
but not my Prince of love and honor
they were not my true love's
my frog who didn't turn into my Prince
I'm hoping I'll find my frog, my Prince
my Prince among men
the one who will cherish the ground I walk on
and be by my side at all times
as I would stand beside him
when he needed me most of all
love makes us do crazy things in life
but if you weren't in love
life would be boring
so what are we gonna do
keep looking for my frog who turns into
my Prince

written: Oct. 17, 2011

Meant To Be

If it is meant to be
then it will be
if not it might
kill me a little inside
and I doubt that I will
ever trust a man again
so very sad, but so very true
I won't push him
into a relationship with me
nope I won't do it
he's gotta want me or leave me
he's gotta want me enough
to stay with me forever
if he can't do that well then
he doesn't deserve me in his life
I will walk away from him
even though I'm dying a slow death inside
gotta wait it out for now
to see what might happen
or won't happen in this lifetime
that's all I can do for now

written: Oct. 19, 2011

Don't Forget To Be Yourself

Don't forget to be yourself
that's what most people
will remember you by
when your gone from there life
she did this or he did that
that's what sets you aside from the others
your ability to do many wonderful things
to be special in the eyes of someone else
your courage to fight your battles in life
and your knowledge to let things go
that you have no control over
we all go through this in life
some more than others in life
life is to short to let things get to you
live life to it's fullest that you can
and never take anything for granted
don't forget to be yourself
that's what most people
will remember you by
when your gone from their life

written: Oct. 20, 2011

Believing

Believing in the unseen
knowing that what you feel
is the greatest thing
you could ever feel in your life
just knowing that it is real
and not something false
you have that sixth sense
about things you believe in
never doubt your belief in anything
once you start doubting you can't quit
you will start doubting everything
and that is not good, it's bad
you'll worry about everything in your life
did I do this right or should I have done that
believing in the unseen
knowing that what you feel
is the greatest thing
you could ever feel in your life

written: Oct. 21, 2011

Waiting My Fate

Waiting my fate
will I get to go home today
or will they keep me longer
with my luck they will keep me longer
I wish he would let me know my fate
instead of keeping me in the dark
I'm freezing cold
all I need is a cold
on top of everything else
they have been so good to me
so I shouldn't complain at all
my nurse's have been great
I will miss them when I leave here
I wish them well all of them
and truly blessed to have met
each and everyone of my nurse's
waiting my fate
will I get to go home today
or will they keep me longer

written: Sept. 26, 2011

Dedicated to the Nurse's
at St. Mary's Hospital

Would You Mind

Would you mind if I said,
"I really want you tonight"
that I truly need you by me
that I need your strength tonight
to make it though the long night
it might not seem long to you
but tonight it feels like forever
forever can be a long time for some
although for others it's no time at all
would you mind if I said,
"I really want you tonight"
that I truly need you by me

written: Sept. 24, 2011

Just A Simple Girl

Just a simple girl
comfortable in shorts or bluejeans
with a t-shirt
I can clean up well
if I need to for some reason
I like being myself though
not some fancy girl
who needs to make an impression
on someone
I'm not a material person
never have been, never will be
I'm happy with who I am
if people can't see what I am
then they are missing the big picture
just a simple girl
comfortable in shorts or bluejeans
with a t-shirt

written: Oct. 23, 2011

What Are The Things
I'm Thankful For

What are the things I'm thankful for
even with a bad heart
God granted me 5 children
3 girls and 2 boys
even tho I don't see them
they are living their dream
I am so proud of them
for going after what they
want in their life
so thankful for the 49 years
I've been granted on this earth
life is so precious and worth living
never take anything for granted
we are not promised a tomorrow
live life to the fullest
go after your dream
and never let anyone tell you
you don't deserve this or that
you deserve the best there is
what are the things I'm thankful for
God granted me life so I might live
and to be a part of something special
I am who I am
nothing more, nothing less

written: Oct. 23, 2011

Lonely

Loneliness has been a part
of my life as far back
as I can remember
even as a child, I felt this way
I carried that loneliness
all through my life
nobody ever knew how I felt
I kept everything locked
up tight in my heart
I refused to let anyone
see how lonely I was
granted I had my 5 children
those days were my
most happiest days ever
but even so, I still felt lonely
starving for friendship
and some that I thought
were my friends, wasn't my friends
they turned on me
I was so disappointed
to learn they had used me
to get what they had wanted
loneliness has been a part
of my life as far back
as I can remember
even now I feel it

written: Oct. 23, 2011

Leaving The Past Behind Me

Leaving the past behind me
I can't change anything now
the memories are still in my head
oh how I wish I could
wipe them out as if
it never even happened
but they will always be there
a part of who I am
and who I am today as a person
that part of my life
will never change
nor will I change
who I am deep down inside
look past the outer body
and look for the good inside me
it is there I promise you
leaving the past behind me
I can't change anything now
I will always & forever be me
just plain & simple me

written: Oct. 23, 2011

Kat Bussell

If You Don't Know Me

If you don't know me by now
how will you ever get to know me
the true me deep down inside
the good-hearted me that I am
the loving side of who I am
time and season separate us
from seeing each other
I so miss seeing you
I've waited my whole life for you
and just when I found you
I lost you again
I'm afraid it just wasn't meant to be
between us, which makes me sad
if you don't know me by now
how will you ever get to know me
I might get a little confused at times
that is not uncommon for some
I am not nor will I ever be perfect
we all make mistakes in life
but unless we spend some time together
how do we know if we are right for each other
if you don't know me by now
how will you ever get to know me
don't give up on me yet
I love you & miss you

written: Oct. 23, 2011

Things Happen

Things happen in life
that's just how it is
maybe it's not what we had planned
but there is a reason for it
and we may not like the end result
but that's just life
you take the good with the bad
and you move on in your life
it may not be easy to move on at first
but in time it get's easier for you
with every step you take
it puts you one step closer to your dream
and that is what is important
gotta hold on to your dreams
work towards something greater
something that stands out from the rest
grab hold of it and never let it go
things happen in life
that's just how it is
maybe it's not what we had planned
but there is a reason for it

written: Oct. 23, 2011

I Want To Hold You Close

I want to hold you close
to me and never let you go
losing you would break my heart in two
oh little one, your more precious
than you'll ever know
I love you more than life
could ever truly give me
I hope you make it back home
where you are loved and cared for

Dedicated to the 10 month old girl
who was taken from her bed
in the middle of the night

written: Oct. 4, 2011

Baby!

Baby, "Where are you?"
your long overdue to be home
I worry so about you
your the first thing I think about
in the morning
and the last thing on my mind
when I lay down at night
if you got hurt
it would hurt me
your the other half of me
that keeps me going through life
baby, "Where are you?"
your long overdue to be home
I worry about you

written: Oct. 4, 2011

Kat Bussell

Nothing Ever Stays The Same

Nothing ever stays the same
even though you wish
you could stop time
and just take the time to enjoy life
and everything around you
beauty isn't just skin deep
it all depends on how you look at beauty
beautiful is not just the outside
appearance
if you watch a sunset, it's beautiful
if you watch the sun come up
it's beautiful
nothing ever stays the same
even though you wish
you could stop time
and just take the time to enjoy life

written: Oct. 4, 2011

It Doesn't Matter

It doesn't matter
who's right or wrong now
the joy of disagreeing
is the making up after wards
loving someone is not always easy
in life or if you're in love
you have to work together
in order for your love
for each other to work
it's not always as easy as it sounds
but if it were easy
would that make a difference to you
would it be worth the risk
of giving your heart to someone else
to loving someone else
who would be willing to invest
in your future together as a couple
it doesn't matter
who's right or wrong now
what are you willing to put into
a relationship with someone new
would you go the distance with them
be their strength when they need you
as they would do for you
it wouldn't take but a second
to make the right choice in life
loving someone is not always easy
but if you work together
oh how wonderful it can be

written: Oct. 4, 2011

75

Past The Point Of Caring

I've gone past the point of caring
I tried many times to make
things right in your life
although, it hasn't done me any good
I feel so unworthy of your trust
for holding love for you
deep down inside my heart
I have always cared about you
even though we weren't together
but receiving love from you
is such a different story
it's as if you have no feelings for me
that you don't care about me
one little bit
this makes me sad
I hope you don't wait to long
to find out what really happened
all those years ago
always remember this,
"I love you!!"

This is for my Kids
written: Oct. 6, 2011

Loving You

Loving you forever, honey
just isn't enough for me
I want it all or nothing
if you can't give me that
then there is no reason
of us being together
I refuse to let a man
break my heart again
loving you forever, honey
just isn't enough for me
I want it all or nothing
I'm not asking for that much
I wanna be me around you
but I also want to be loved
I want you to be you
when we are together
loving you forever, honey
just isn't enough for me
I want it all or nothing

Inspired by: Kiss's song: Forever
written: Oct. 8, 2011

Kat Bussell

Life Is So Complicated

Life is so complicated
I never thought it'd be this way
when I pictured my life
with my soul-mate it was
a completely different story
but then things started changing
I didn't know how to stop it
then one day I fell out of love
with him & his way of life
I wanted more than what I got
out of our so-called life together
life is so complicated
I never thought it'd be this way
life can be so cruel to you
things you thought were behind you
always come forward in your life
they can ruin your life forever
why do things have to change
why do people have to change
what's wrong with you
just being yourself in life
life is so complicated
I never thought it'd be this way

written: Oct. 8, 2011

The Other Side

I crossed to the other side
I went through the door
not knowing what or who waited for me
but I did it, I opened that door
and stepped through anyway
but the greatest part is I didn't
look back, I kept going never to return
leaving wasn't easy for me
but it was way past time to
move on with my life
to make my life better for me
as long as I can do so
I will cross through that door
to the other side of what, I don't know
no looking back now it's done & over
only moving forward with my life & needs
I crossed to the other side
I went through the door
not knowing what or who waited for me

written: Nov. 24, 2011

How Many Times

How many times
is it gonna take me
to learn my lesson
that not everyone loves
with their heart
I keep saying just one more time
just one more time
and every time I get my heart broke
what is wrong with me
it's time to realize that, I'm unlovable
it's hopeless to dream
that there is someone out there for me
so tired of dreaming
that he is out their somewhere
looking for me
how many times
is it gonna take me
to learn my lesson

written: Oct. 8, 2011

Flying Away

I may not have the best life
nor a good man at my side
but what I do have is God & family
even though my heart is dying
one day I will be flying away
to a place of no more pain
I won't have to worry about my
heart stopping to beat anymore
cause when I fly away
I won't have to suffer any more
I may not have the best life
nor a good man at my side
but what I do have is God & family
so when the time comes
for me to leave this world behind
do not be sad for me
but rejoice in all we have been
through together over the years
rejoice in the fact that all my pain
will be behind me, forever and ever
but my heart will always be here with you
to show you what love is all about
it got lost down the highway of life
people forgot how to love one and another

written: Dec. 7, 2011
at 10:26 pm

Walking Thru Life

Walking thru life, wondering
what does it hold for me
will I ever be 100% happy
or will I wear a frown forever
and feeling so out of place
in a world full of people
who are happy & in love
what is my purpose here
what do I need to do
in order to be 100% happy
please tell me what I'm doing wrong
so I can correct the problem
not knowing what I've done wrong
is eating away at me
walking thru life, wondering
what does it hold for me
walking thru life, wondering
always wondering what I did wrong

written: Oct. 9, 2011

Lonesome

Lonesome is what so many
people go through a lot these days
that wasn't what they had wanted
but fate wasn't as kind to them
things they wanted just didn't work out
the way they had wanted
them to work out
oh how I understand that feeling
I have the same problem
fate wasn't as kind to me either
lonesome is what so many
people go through a lot these days
even though I cherish my freedom
I miss all those little things
that go with being in love
that so many people take for granted
oh how I wish I had
those little things again
I would never take them
for granted again
lonesome is what so many
people go through a lot these days

written: Oct. 8, 2011

You May Not Miss Me

You may not miss me now
but sometime in the near future
you just might think of me
and wish upon a star
that she would come back to me
I didn't know what I had
at that point in my life
until I realized what I lost
and then it was already to late
she has moved on without me
in her life, good—bye honey
you may not miss me now
but sometime in the near future
you just might think of me
I wish I could go back in time
and rewrite my future
and include her into it
but that is only a passing fantasy now
she left me and didn't look back
oh how I made a mistake
you may not miss me now
but sometime in the near future
you just might think of me

written: Oct. 10, 2011
Inspired by: You'll Think Of Me
by: Keith Urban

God Give Me

God give me a man
who is worthy of my time
and of my undying love
and who will respect me
enough to be kind & gentle
enough to really care about me
God grant me the wisdom
to treat him with respect
enough to be kind & gentle
to show compassion when
the need comes for it
and that he can trust me
for every need that comes
our way in life
and that I can trust him
with my life and love
God give me a man
who is worthy of my time
and of my undying love

written: Oct. 11, 2011

Inspired by: Heaven
by: The Los Lonely Boys

Just A Fool

Just a fool to think
that someone could love her
love sucks at times
or maybe she is a witch
dressed in nice cloths
pretending to be something she is not
so she can drag the guy in
to loving her forever
only she is not what he thought
she had lied to get him
and now he wonders how to get out
of the mess he now see's himself in
just now realizing he could never love her
the way she wants to be loved
just a fool to think
that someone could love her
he is the perfect man she tells herself
so she goes all out to make him believe
they are meant to be together
til the end of time
he tries to believe what she says
but he just can't do that
not after what he has seen
he deserves something better
than what she can offer him
just a fool to think
that someone could love her

written: Oct. 27, 2011

Just Don't Give Up

Just don't give up
it's there just dig deeper
you'll find it soon
just a little deeper
I promise it is there
just don't give up
on me it's there
I'll let you know
if you hurt me, promise
I'll grab the bedside rail
if it hurts to much
just don't give up, Nurse
it's there just dig deeper

written: Oct. 14, 2011

Find Me A Preacher

Find me a preacher
let's say, "I do"
and live happily ever after
oh honey lets do this
do you really want to be alone
for the rest of your life
I know for certain I don't
so will you say yes
I'd say yes in a heartbeat
if you asked me to be yours
every day with you would be paradise
for the rest of our lives
because we would be together
find me a preacher
let's say, "I do"
and live happily ever after
what do you have to lose
look at all you gain
me loving you forever

written: Oct. 26, 2011

Inspired by: Cheap Trick
Don't Be Cruel

Don't Crush Me

Don't crush me
don't crush what spirit
I have left, honey
not sure I could make
it through this time
it would leave me wounded
broken—hearted, dead inside
I've been there before
and I don't want
to feel that way again
I'd never do anything
to hurt you, promise
Honey, I love you
you never hurt the one you love
don't crush me
don't crush what spirit
I have left, honey
I just want you to love me
as I love you, honey
let's give it a try
what do you say
are you a willing person
to give us a try

written: Oct. 26, 2011

I Want You

I want you, need you, love you
can't live without you
tell me you want me too
that you don't think you
can live without me
I need you to want me
do I need to shed some tears
so I can get my way
oh Lord, I'd never do that
not even to you, dear
even though I love you so
forcing you into anything
would be selfish & unkind
I'm not that type of person
I want you, need you, love you
can't live without you
but if I can't have you
in time I will understand
I hope that if you don't
want me, that we can
still be friends forever more
even though I love you so

written: Oct. 26, 2011

Inspired by: Cheap Trick
I Want You To Want Me

Cheaters & Cheating

Men & women alike cheat
on their spouse's, thinkin'
who am I hurting anyway
no one will ever find out
what I'm doing, so it's okay
not everyone is like this, in life
most think they will never get caught
but in the end they do get caught
and they will lie to your face about it
come on now, get real here
who is gonna respect you after you
do such a thing as cheating
you've ruined your marriage or
your relationship you had
for whatever reason you did it
this kind of pain, makes it hard for
anyone to trust you again
trust along with love, respect & kindness
is what it takes to make or break
your marriage or relationship
without these in your life

your history in the eyes of the one
who loves you more than life itself
is it really worth cheating
everything you had is gone
in the blink of an eye
your just now realizing that you lost
the best thing you ever had
but you realized to late
the damage is done
very seldom is it fixable

written: Oct. 26, 2011
a friend asked me to write about this
I've been there, I know how it feels

The Webs Of A Dreamer

What dream do you want to
dream about tonight, dear
a night of hot steaming passion
building around us a web of many dreams
built in the stages of loving you
nothing is hard when you are near me
I lose my mind when you are close
what dream do you want to
dream about tonight, dear
a night of cuddling close
a romantic movie before we go to bed
or a night of melting romance
the kind that just makes you
weak in your legs and your not sure
if they will hold you up or you
will fall to the floor in a puddle
what dream do you want to
dream about tonight, dear

written: Oct. 29, 2011

Surprise Me, Baby

Surprise me, Baby
do something unexpected
show me that you care
what are you gonna do to
surprise me, baby
I'm waiting to see what you got
up your sleeve tonight
will I be surprised
at what you will do tonight
surprise me, baby
do something to make me tingle
that sends shivers down my spine
that I never knew you could do
make me love you so much more
surprise me, baby
what will you do baby?
To show me you love me
I hope it excites me down to the bone
I can't wait to see what you'll do next
surprise me, baby
surprise me, baby
surprise me, baby

written: Dec. 25, 2011
at 2:21 am

Inspired by: Tommy Thayer
singing: Shock Me

So Easy

It's so easy to fall in love {x2}
you can fall in love at first sight
without knowing anything about
that person at all
love can make you do things
you never thought possible
love is great at times
but it can also crush you too
if your not careful
some love with their whole heart
others pretend to love you
so they can get what they want
then dump you in a heartbeat
it's so easy to fall in love {x2}
you can fall in love at first sight
without knowing anything about
that person at all
if you find your perfect soul-mate
life can be so precious
you just wanna hold on tight

and never let go of the best thing
you have ever found
I will always & forever love you
from the bottom of my heart
to the top of my heart
it's so easy to fall in love {x2}
you can fall in love at first sight
without knowing anything about
that person at all
you just know deep down inside you
they are the one your to love
til the end of time
it's so easy to fall in love {x3}

written: Oct. 30, 2011

Tangled Up In You

Tangled up in you
your all I ever think about now
since you have walked back
into my life again
time & distance was between us
from the beginning
we went our separate ways
doing what we had to do back then
we never had a chance back then
fate is now giving us that
to see if we would be right
for each other
tangled up in you
your all I ever think about now
since you have walked back
into my life again
I wonder if we will ever find out
if we were meant to be together
so much stands between us now
your job and my not having a way
to you so we can be together
if only for a short time
any time with you would be worth
a million great memories
tangled up in you
your all I ever think about
since you have walked back
into my life again

written: Oct. 14, 2011

Enjoying My Time

Enjoying my stay at the Hilton Hospital
the Hilton hospital can be whatever
you want it to be, a place of rest
and being waited on hand and foot
they help you whenever you need help
all you have to do is ask for help
the Nurse's are nice, polite and curtious
I would rate my care at or over a 10
my private room is nice
I can watch anything I want
and not worry if my room mate likes
what I'm watching or when I watch it
enjoying my stay at the Hilton Hospital
all you have to do is use your imagination
it can take you to places you've never been
granted it might be a dream fantasy
but it's your dream and why not use it
for something so wonderful
instead of dreaming of something terrible
that will haunt you forever
there is no fun in that
enjoying my stay at the Hilton Hospital

written: Oct. 15, 2011

He Came To See Me

My farmer boy came to see me
while I was staying at the hospital
it so made my day
I'd sent him my room number
but wasn't sure if he'd come to see me
oh so wished he could of stayed a little longer
he's so handsome, it should be outlawed
I just can't resist his charm
that school boy charm, get's to me
every time, melts my heart
and I just want to hold on to him
so afraid he will go away
and that I will never see him again
that would be a terrible shame to lose
they say it's better to love and lose
than to never be loved at all
my farmer boy came to see me
while I was staying at the hospital
it so made my day

written: Oct. 15, 2011

You Say It Best

You say it best
when you take me in your arms
and smile down at me
as I look up into your eyes
I just know you won't let me fall
you'd be there to catch me
if I should fall
you'd reach out and take my hand
to help me up should I ever fall
you say it best
when you take me in your arms
and smile down at me
as I look up into your eyes
I believe I'm falling for you
falling in love that is, with you
you've brought so much back
into my life, things I thought
were dead inside me,
but has come back to life
inside of me, the true person
that I am and was at one time
I'm so glad you came back into my life
you say it best
when you take me into your arms
and smile down at me
as I look up into your eyes

written: Oct. 15, 2011

Tropical Paradise #2

Tropical paradise #2 at
the Hilton Hospital
search your mind for that
special place that you've always
wanted to go, a tropical paradise
I'm at that tropical paradise
in my mind more than my body is
maybe some day I can go to
that tropical paradise for real
but if I never make it there
I have been there in my imagination
at the Hilton Hospital
see that's the nice thing about
dreaming you can do anything you want to
be anybody you want to be
while there in your imagination
that's what people don't think about
where could I go and what could I do
while there enjoying the beauty
that surrounds you everywhere
tropical paradise #2 at
the Hilton Hospital
search your mind for that
special place that you've always
wanted to go, a tropical paradise

written: Oct. 15, 2011

What's Your Dream

What's your dream
what do you want more than anything
to be accepted for who I am
to be loved for who I am
to be understood for who I am
what's your dream
what do you want more than anything
to not hurt anymore body wise
or heart wise
I've takin' a beatin' but
I'm still here for a reason
I don't know why, but I just know
how I feel inside
and with that you can accomplish
anything your heart desires what's your dream
what do you want more than anything

written: Oct. 15, 2011

To Catch A Falling Star

To catch a falling star
tonite I plan to catch a
falling star in my hand
dreaming of what a star looks like
and how it would feel in my hands
what a dream this would be
but you can dream big
don't ever let anything stop you
from what you want
go after that falling star
reach out and grab it
to catch a falling star
tonite I plan to catch a falling star
in the palm of my hands
oh what a great feelin' that would be
to hold a star in the palm of your hands
to catch a falling star
tonite I plan to catch one
and make it mine for all eternity

written: Oct. 15, 2011

Elizabeth

Elizabeth oh Elizabeth
your a wonderful nurse
a treasure to your profession
you should be honored for who
you are, my dear nurse
you deserve better than
what you have gotten
for a job well done
you kept your calm
during a storm
you didn't see it comin'
you did the right thing
you asked for help to deal
with your pain
when you really needed it
Elizabeth oh Elizabeth
your a wonderful nurse
a treasure to your profession

written: Oct. 15, 2011

Heaven

I hope to walk the streets
of Heaven someday
I wanna see the streets of gold
and see my father there
I know it wasn't easy for you
but my love for you is real
I miss you so, I wish you were still here
I hope to walk the streets
of Heaven someday
I can imagine it's beautiful
more precious than anything
we have ever seen in our life time
although I'm in no hurry to join you
I do miss you so and all that you
have missed in my life and meeting
your grand kids before you left that night
I hope to walk the streets
of Heaven someday
I wanna see the streets of gold

written. Nov. 1, 2011

Dedicated to: Marion Williams

105

I'm Letting Go

I'm letting go
of the most important
thing in my life
my three older children
as much as this hurts me
I don't have much choice
they refused to contact me
I've begged & tried my best
to see them & nothing
no contact back from them
life sucks sometimes
I love them with all my heart
but there is a time
when you just gotta let go
I'm letting go
of the most important
thing in my life
my three older children
I hope & pray that they will
one day find out the truth
of what happened so long ago
I was dragged thru the mud and muck
turned into some kind of monster
those who truly knew me should of known better
but they believed the lies spread about me
which hurt to the core of my being
how could anyone be so cruel

written: Oct. 15, 2011

The Hospital Kitten

The Hospital kitten
a small gray calico kitten
much like my Queenie & Mickie
Queenie had to be put down
when she was about 3 months old
she came in contact with a tick
off of a bobcat
of course it nearly killed me
to put her down she was in so
much pain I just couldn't let her
suffer any more than she had been
she was so beautiful
I loved her to death, she was my baby
I still miss her to this day
but I know she will not have to suffer anymore
Mickie I had to leave behind
with my ex-boyfriend cause I didn't
have room for her in my Mom's van
that nearly killed me, I loved her so too
the hospital kitten isn't as dark in color
as mine were but still a very cute kitten
in her own right, she was made perfect
but someone who loves animals
the way I do will love any animal

written: Oct. 15, 2011

My Life

My life is an open book
one that is good & bad
life has been hard on me
but I refuse to give up
I pick myself up & move on
honestly that's all you can do these days
just as anyone else would do
life is a struggle for us all at times
but that is what makes us stronger
as a person who is unwilling to give up
the fight for what's right in their life
even though it doesn't feel that way
you have to believe in yourself
and say "I can do this"
don't ever back down, cause then
they have you right where they want you
tell yourself, "I can do anything I set out to do"
nothing or no one is gonna drag me down
life is good if you want it to be
if you don't want it good
then I truly feel sorry for you
because you will never be happy
things in your life will never change
and they will drag you down so much
that you begin to believe you are worthless
and that is a horrible way to live life

written: Jun. 22, 2011

Inspired by: Shawn Malcolm

Miles Between Us

We have miles & miles between us
oh how I wish we didn't
but the fact is we do
we went our separate ways
as mine took me away from you
yours took you away from me
those years lost to us
that we can never get back
I wonder if we had or ever had a chance
maybe we would still be together today
and so totally happy with our life together
why oh why did you have to come
back into my life now and of all things tell me,
"You had one major crush on me"
why didn't you ever tell me this before
our lives could have been so different
than what they are today, lonely
will this work between us now, I so want it too
I have lost my heart to you
I have fallen in love with you
anything else just won't do
we deserve to find happiness
even if it is in the arms of each other
you make me feel alive again and I was afraid,
I'd never feel that way again ever
to live a life of loneliness
was what I thought I deserved
now I know that isn't the case anymore
I love you!!

written: Jun. 23, 2011

Putting My Heart On The Line

I'm putting my heart on the line for you
I'm willing to sacrifice my heart
just one more time, for you
please don't let me down like all the others
life has been one disappointment
after another in my life
men who I thought truly loved me for who I was
what a joke I turned out to be for them
they never loved me, just used me
to get what they wanted out of life
they got everything they wanted
and took everything else that meant
the world to me, they didn't care
how much they hurt me
as long as they got what they wanted
that's all that mattered to them
I'm putting my heart on the line for you
I'm willing to sacrifice my heart
just one more time, for you
please don't let me down like all the others
life has been one disappointment
after another in my life

written; Jun. 23, 2011

Listen With Your Heart

Listen with your heart
it will guide you down the right path
your heart will let you know when it's right
all you gotta do is listen
true love is given only once in a lifetime
so you need to be prepared for
anything that comes along
who knows you just might find it one more time
but you gotta love with your whole heart
if you expect it to work out between you
and the person you have fallen in love with
it takes a 100% from both people to
you make the relationship work
without it you might as well be
on a sinking boat, cause you will fail
the test of time with the one you love
more than living life and being
just down right miserable
listen to your heart
it will guide you down the right path
your heart will let you know when it's right
all you gotta do is listen
listen to your heart
it will guide you down the right path
your heart will let you know when it's right
all you gotta do is listen

Kat Bussell

You Know It's Not

You know it's not
a broken heart
that bothers me
it's the thought of
being alone for the
rest of my life
broken hearts come
a dime a dozen
I've had mine broke
so many times
I quit counting them
it's just the facts of life
you learn to live
with the fact that
people just don't
care who they hurt
you know it's not
a broken heart
that bothers me
when you love
someone you love
them when all else
tells you it's hopeless
that's how life is
either you love someone
or you don't love them
you know it's not
a broken heart
that bothers me

written: Nov. 14, 2011

Walking Away

My mother fell tonight
I couldn't get to her fast enough
she refused to let us help her
so in anger, I unleashed my mouth
saying words in anger only makes
things worse in your life
you live to regret them, someday
and they will haunt you forever
I stopped myself, bit my tongue
and turned away from her
hurt by the fact she wouldn't
let me help her get up
I walked away from her
before I could say anything else
that I would regret later in life
I left the house to get away
to calm down and to be alone to write
but my inspiration just
isn't working the way I want
I have so much pulling at me
I don't know where to start
and now this on top of everything else
makes things even worse for me
I want to run away and hide
from the world and
everything that haunts me

written: Oct. 31, 2011

Can I Keep You

Can I keep you, my dear
you make me who I am
I so love that about being with you
I feel so alive again
that's something I haven't felt in years
I thought you were my Prince Charming
you just re-entered my life
after going our separate ways in life
my ideas of Prince Charming have changed
not sure if he even exists
at least not for me anyway
can I keep you, my dear
you make me who I am
I so love that about being with you
I doubt I will ever find my
Prince Charming
the man I am to love forever
I feel lost & lonely again
what am I doing wrong
am I unlovable
all I can say is, "I must be."

written: Oct. 31, 2011

To All My Online Sisters

I love you all
as if we were borne
from the same parents
I have been blessed
to have you in my life
and hope you feel the same
I hate to think of what
my life would have been
had we all never meet
so in saying that
I am so glad we all meet
even if it is over a computer
I treasure every minute
of our time together
may we have many more
years together as sisters
sisters forever!

written: Nov. 6, 2011

The Most Amazing Night

Life is never what you think
around every corner there is
a new experience waiting for you
and a new friend to add to those
you already cherish more than life
what a perfect gift anyone could
ever truly want out of life
the most amazing night
I feel so blessed to have a life
filled with so many amazing people
people I consider family & friends
what could be better than that
life is never what you think
around every corner there is
a new experience waiting for you
life for me was just an empty existence
walking one day to the next day
but all that has changed for me
life now has meaning for me
and worth living every new day
getting up to say, "Hi" to my
sisters & friends online
oh wow, how amazing is that
life is never what you think
around every corner there is
a new experience waiting for you

written: Nov. 6, 2011

Lonely Is Real

Lonely is real
it's the worse part of life
when you have no one
to care about you
you really don't know
till you've been there
you feel lost along with
being lonely in life
yes, it is sad to say
but there are so many
people out there who are lonely
and have no one to love
them or even show that
they care about you
really care about you
it is sad to live that way in life
most don't have a choice
it's been a way of life for so long
they don't know any other way to live
lonely is real
it's the worst part of life
when you have no one
to care about you

written: Nov. 7, 2011

117

The Facts Of Life

The facts of life
no matter how bad you
want something
some things just aren't
meant to be
and yes it hurts you
but you shake it off
you still have your pride,
your dignity & self worth
you can & will survive
because I am worth more
than what you think I am
take off your blinders and
look at me as a person
what do you see in me
am I worth your time
and effort you spend on me
the facts of life
no matter how bad you
want something
some things just aren't
meant to be

written: Nov. 9, 2011

You Gotta Love Me, Forever

You gotta love me, forever
Lord, knows I will always & forever
love you
yes, we may have some rough times in life
that is a part of life, honey
but we can work them out together as a team
loving someone is sharing the rough
times in life just as much as the good times
they will simply go away if we work together
let's give it a chance to see if it will work out
you gotta love me, forever
Lord knows I will always & forever
love you
let's build a treasure
of loving each other
and spending the rest of
our time together and
not alone in life
Lord, knows I will always & forever
love you, honey

written: Nov. 9, 2011

Just A Drop In The Bucket

A broken heart is just
a drop in the bucket
men like that come a dime
a dozen
they don't care about how they
make you feel all they care about
are themselves and getting what they want
then you came along
and changed my whole life
and my idea's of what Prince Charming
should be like to the woman he loves & care's about
and now I'm not for sure
what is real and what is not real
I'm confused as to what you want
what you need out of a woman
a broken heart is just
a drop in the bucket
men like that come a dime a dozen
they just don't care about you anymore
I love you, but I'm not sure
if that's enough to keep you
a broken heart is just
a drop in the bucket
men like that come a dime a dozen

written: Nov. 11, 2011

Angels

Angels are the most precious
of all the people in the world
they have been sent to watch over you
to give you comfort when it is needed
all you have to do is believe in them
you are special to your maker
he brought you into this world
and he takes us out when it is time
for us to start a new journey
do not be afraid to believe
Angels are the most precious
of all the people in the world
they have been sent to watch over you
to give you comfort when it is needed
in something you can't see
he is their for you when you need him
he is never far from us ever
I take comfort in knowing that I have
angels watching over me daily
even if I can't see them
I know they are near me always
Angels are the most precious
of all the people in the world
they have been sent to watch over you
to give you comfort when it is needed
Angels are the most precious
of all the people in the world
they have been sent to watch over you
to give you comfort when it is needed

written: Apr. 25, 2012
at 12:57 am

121

I Have Better Things

I have better things to do
than think about you
I have a life to live
and you won't be a part of it, honey
it's what you chose
it's not what I wanted
I have better things to do
than think about you
I have a life to live
things to do that's important to me
I'm not giving up on my dreams
it's mine and I want it
more than anything else
I love you & will miss you
while I'm gone
you will always be in my heart
and if you can't wait for me
then it wasn't meant to be
for us to be together
I love you & will miss you
I have better things to do
than think about you
I have a life to live

written: Nov. 16, 2011

A Great Friend
{Delilah}

Your body is gone
but your heart & soul
linger on through those
who knew you best
so be troubled not
my family cause
even though I am gone
my heart & soul lives on
through you the ones
I loved with all my heart
don't cry and be sad
over me cause I am in
a better place now
what a loss to the world
so much knowledge to share
with whoever would listen
I will miss you my dear friend
but I know you are
in a better place now
where you know no pain
no suffering from sickness
your body is gone
but your heart & soul
linger on through those
who knew you best

written: Nov. 2, 2011

Name changed due to keep the privacy
of the person this poem is about private

Kat Bussell

Encouragement

One needs a lot of encouragement
to survive in this world we live in
there are those who love to control you

For those who are abused
you have to find the courage to
stand up against controlling people
if you look deep into your heart
you can & will find that courage
it's there inside you even though
you can't feel it there anymore
you've been beaten so much that
it's hard to find happiness in life
never give up, find your happiness
and when you find that you can withstand
anything that comes your way

For you who have been sexually abused
God knows you did not deserve what
happen to you, it destroys who you are
as a person and how you live life after
being attacked by a unknown person
your threatened to keep this a secret
and if you tell you will be hurt the next time
you have to find that courage inside you
you can't continue to live in fear
of what tomorrow brings

Find the courage to stand up for yourself
take back your life, change your destiny

No – one deserves to be unhappy!!!!

written: Nov. 9, 2002

124

Nothing Is Out Of Reach

Nothing is out of reach
if you want it bad enough
you have to have faith and
reach out & grab it

Sit down and make you a list
of goals you want to accomplish
then when you achieve your goals
check them off one by one

Their will be some who do
not know this due process
so we need to teach them
what you have learned

Their will be some who
will not like the changes in you
and believe me I know that to be fact
but so what
as long as your happy who cares

There is always someone out there in this world who
is sad & depressed and wants there life to end
don't end your life, that's not the answer. That's
very much how I felt way back then.
There is help out there, you just have to look for it.
Nothing is out of reach. You deserve to be happy
no matter who thinks what about you.
Grab at the life you want, not the life someone else
thinks you should have.

Written: Nov. 10, 2002

Fight Harder

I know how hard it is to fight harder
sometimes it feels almost impossible
just when you think your getting ahead
they send you back five steps

I have been there many times in my life
no matter how hard you try in life
it just isn't good enough for them

I was once a strong person years ago
but I've been put down so much
by family & so-called friends in my life
I lost my will to fight back

but now I'm regaining my strengths
I'm not giving up the fight yet
I'm gonna fight till the end no matter what
I'm not giving up this time
I will win this battle

written: Nov. 13, 2002

I Must Admit I Never Thought Until Now

My whole childhood & adult life has
been run by someone else
you do this, you do that, you'll do as I say
someone's always telling you what to do
and if you don't do it, you're in trouble
everyone seems to think they are your boss
so I feel like a puppet on a string
I must admit I never thought until now
I learned a valuable lesson
I don't have to do what everyone says
who died and made them God?
It feels great to be able to think again
the most amazing happy thoughts
life has meaning again, since
I learned a valuable lesson

written; Nov. 14, 2002

I learned this my last day in a Mental Hospital
it was the only way I could continue to live life as I knew it,
now I live life how I want to live it
and well, if people don't like it or the new me
who cares, "I'm happy," for the first time in my life!!!

With Every Trial

Everyone's life is set on a trial
that some want to change, but can't
because of the life they lead

with every new trial
comes a great responsibility
to achieve your goals you set
one must learn and live

with your life there is always something
new that comes your way
you must learn to deal with it
in the only way you know how to do

whether it be your children,
your husband or maybe even your
beloved parents, bless their hearts
everyone has something in life to deal with

learn to live with your everyday trails
if you don't your life will never be
a normal life at all, it can & will be misery

Your life will be a sticky mess of webs
that will always seem to double in size
instead of decreasing in size

Get your life back & be happy
learn to deal with the trials in your life
if you don't deal with them, who will
and you will be angry at everything & everyone

written: Jun. 16, 2003

No More

When you can't take anymore
you just have to say, "No more."
if you let it continue to go on
you just have to stop and think
what is going on here
you're not my boss

on the other hand
life can be so grand
that you feel as if you could fly
anything is possible if you want it bad enough

on the other hand
life can be so terrible that
sometimes you just want to die
because you just can't take it anymore

you have to learn to say, "No more."
I'm not taking it anymore
that I deserve better than that
just stop and say, "No more."

Everyone deserves to be happy
just once in there life
and hope that, that happiness
last forever and ever

written: Nov. 14, 2002

Who Is My Destiny?

Who is my destiny
the one I'm to love forever
please send me a sign
will he love me forever
like I will love him
with all my heart
my destiny will change my
life forever with his love
please send me a sign
will we have a lot in common
will we share our hearts
till the day we die
will we share an
eternity together
please send me a sign
I wish upon a star for
my one true destiny
with all my heart
till the day we leave this earth
and enter the gates of Heaven
please send me a sign

written: May 2005

Love Hurts

Love hurts when your not looking
you think you can trust a person
who tells you, "I love you,"
but then goes behind your back
and see's another
which destroys your dream,
your heart breaks in half, torn
you find it hard to trust another
with fear it will happen again
is the pain from a broken heart
worth going through it again
it's a chance we all take in life
if you turn love away
love will turn you away in the end
not everyone is dishonest
love does hurt when your not looking
you think you can trust a person
who tells you, "I love you."
They only say the words to make you happy
and so you will leave them alone
I wasn't borne yesterday
and I'm far from being stupid

written: Nov. 18, 2005

Inside

Look inside the person
for the beauty lays beneath the surface
not the outside appearance
a kind giving heart is the true
treasure of the person they are
look inside yourself and see
if you have the kind, caring heart
in order to understand a person
you must look at the inside of that person
what is that person willing to do for another
asking for nothing in return except for a smile
will you take the time it requires
to look deep down inside the person
for whom you care about
or will you go for the outside appearance
missing the true person they are
appearances can be deceiving
for this you must look closely for
what's on the inside

written: Nov. 19, 2005

Marked For Love

Remember John 3:16
God gave his son's life for our sins
we are marked for love
God has given you his love
we must be willing to accept it
would you be willing to accept
his love for you
I'm willing to receive his love
I'm willing to let him
into my life, to love me
show me the way through life's
dark lonely valley's
comfort me when I realize
things are to rough for me
guide me when all I want
to do is give up
love me when I feel
no–one else does

written: Nov. 20, 2005

inspired by: Pastor Jack Blansit

Miles Of Trouble

I have miles of trouble
with no chance of success
every time I think I get
one step forward
I go back three steps
and have to start over again
when will I see the light of day
will my bad luck ever leave me
everyone makes mistakes
it's a part of life
you learn from them
and move on with your life
when will people forgive me
of my mistakes
still trying to figure out what I did wrong
why am I being blamed for everything
let it go and let me move on with my life
it feels like they want to destroy me
as if my ex-husband hadn't done enough to me
left alone and so very unhappy with life

written: Dec. 11, 2005

The Best Of My Love

You get the best of my love
my love that is honest & sincere
you'll never find someone,
who will love you as much as I do
you're the one I've been waiting for
for all my life
where have you been hiding
you get the best of my love
my love that is honest & sincere
your the light of my life
the torch that leads me thru
the dark tunnels in my life
oh how lost I'd be
lost without you at my side
you get the best of my love
my love that is honest & sincere

written: Dec. 16, 2005

Love At Last

Wipe the eyes, put on a smile
cause, "I love you."
your gonna see the poet
in me yet, "Babe"
it's okay to be emotional
that's what shows we are human
I'm there with you in your heart
even though you can't feel me
this is good, this is right
when you finally look
into my eyes
you will know that,
"I love you."
more than life itself

written: Dec. 23, 2005

The Broken Heart

Once upon a time, long, long ago
I had a whole heart
but, I trusted a man who
I thought had truly loved me
I so learned a harder than hard lesson
he took everything from me
my kids, my home and left my heart broken
he remarried shortly after he divorced me
I waited 4 months before I remarried
to another man who I believed loved me
oh boy, what a mistake I had made
he hid his criminal past from me
had no idea he had a criminal record
he flirted with women in front of me
and I shouldn't have to tell you how that hurt
it broke my heart in two
how could anyone say, "I do"
and then do that to his wife
two very hard lessons
and even though it took me a long
time to forgive them
it made it hard for me to trust again
not everyone gives love with
there whole heart, so as you can tell
I ended having my heart broken two times
the broken heart
will it ever be able to trust again
I think not!!

written: Jan. 14, 2006

Lost Hope

The struggles of everyday life are
getting harder by the day & night
getting out of bed is almost a chore
I don't want to get up everyday
but, I make myself get up
trying to hold on to the hope
I carry within me, which is almost gone
my lost hope is dying in me
no matter how hard I try
it's never good enough for others
Me a sweet, kind, and caring person
is being beat down by others
saying, "I'm bad for my kids."
the struggles of everyday life are
getting harder by the day & night

written: May 30, 2006

My Idea Of A Perfect Man

1} He must be honest & sincere

2} he must be willing to make a commitment

3} he would look deeply into my eyes & see
my love for him only

4} he would tell me, "I love you," and mean it

5} he must bring me Orange Roses after we've fought

6} that he would never grow tired of kissing me

7} he would whisper sweet nothings in my ears

8} we would share about our days at the end of the night

9} that he would hold me through the night

10} he would call me, "Sweetheart"

written: Jun. 1, 2006

No Heart Of Stone

I've no heart of stone
like some people I know
to have a heart of stone
means you care about no-one but yourself
how pitiful does that make you
that's pretty bad in my books
I can say, "I care about others feelings."
I've no heart of stone
like some people I know
life sometimes is very hard
sometimes it's so hard it stinks
but honestly, "Life is what you make of it."
It's never to late you can change
your heart of stone
all you need is kindness & compassion
and a listening ear, your problems
in life, may not be as bad as
someone else's problems

written: Jun. 18, 2006

Bottled Up Emotions

It's so easy to bottle up your emotions
in your mind, hiding how you feel
no–body knows how unhappy you are
it's easy to shut people out, this way
you don't have to worry about being
hurt again, until recently my whole
life had been that way
now I know how to deal with the
way people make me feel, I have
control of my life, if people don't
like the "New me," so what
the only person I have to please is me

written: Jun. 19, 2006

No End To My Struggles

I've done everything I can do
to the best of my ability
I've lived my life doing everything
every one else wants me to do
it's still not enough for them
I can see no end to my struggles
everything I do is never enough
"When is to much, really to much?"
they have run me into the ground
saying, "I'm the one who is bad for my kids."
what is left to hope for, when so many people
are dead set against you? Hope has come and
gone in my life, my lost hope.
Do you know what it's like missing your children?
Them growing up without you in there life
lost years with my kids that I can never
get back. I can see no end to my struggles. To my lost hope . . .

written: Jun 20, 2006

Angels Lookin' Over You!

Angels do indeed exist
all you have to do is believe
with all your heart
that they do indeed exist
on this earth
they are chosen especially for you
to protect you from bodily harm
God put us here for a reason
to live the life he wanted you to have
he did not intend for your life
to be cut short on this earth
for any reason
so live the life God wanted you to have
cause you have Angels lookin' over you!

Written: Jul. 14, 2006

Inspired by: Kathe Posadas

One Day Soon

My hearts desire will happen
one day soon
a good hearted man, to love
a home to share our love
for each other in
to love, honor & cherish
till death do we part
one day soon everything
will fall into place
as God had planned for me
before I was conceived
in my mother's womb
although, the waiting
has been hard for me
I will not give up
on my hope, that my
desire's will be met in time
my hearts desire will
happen one day soon
I will be waiting for it to happen

written: Jul.20, 2006

Two Ships Passing In The Night

Two ships passing in the night
that's what we are, babe
two lonely people searching
for their one true love
in the vast world which we live in
two people passing each other and
never truly seeing each other
when will our ships collide
will our love for each other
survive the test of time
I hope so, I'm tired of being
lonely, the rest of my life
I wish to share my love with you babe
two ships passing in the night
that's what we are, babe

written: Jul. 26, 2006

There Is A Fire Burning
In My Heart For You

There is a fire burning in my heart for you
a fire of love burning so warm, gentle & patient
you have no idea the effect you have over me
there is a fire burning in my heart for you
the sight of your strong hard body, just
waiting for me to wrap my arms
around you & to kiss those
luscious lips of yours
oh babe, you were made
just for me to love
there is a fire burning in my heart,
soul & mind
please tell me you love me as much
I love you with all my heart

written : Jul.27, 2006

got this poem one night, when the Napoleon, MO
fire truck was responding to a fire call

A Long Lost Love

A long lost love forgotten
due to an unknown letter
that no-one knows anything about
Shaun claims that Penny wrote him
a dear John letter
that sent two hearts adrift into the arms
of a stranger to receive comfort from
the deep hurt in their hearts from this
so-called letter has brought them great pain
each have suffered because of this letter
both took different paths down life's long road
a long lost love that still to this day thrives for each other
but they are committed to the spouse they find
themselves married to, this is love
a love that has and will endure the test of time
maybe one day they can share that love & share their
lives as one, as it should have been in the beginning,
but got sidetracked along the way
hopefully true love will conquer this time
for Shaun & Penny
a long lost love forgotten

written: Jul. 20, 2006

Name's have been changed for privacy
of the 2 people the poem is about

My Singing Heart

My singing heart is calling
out to your heart
a tune of love to reach the
heaven's and beyond
my willing heart is waiting for
a response from my handsome guy
a romantic dinner for two
waiting to be eaten
a midnight stroll under
the neon yellow moon
my singing heart is calling
out to your heart
will I hear what I'm waiting to hear?

Written: Jul.28, 2006

The Woods

The many trees surrounding the property
full of lush green leaves everywhere you look
paths made to streams that snake through
the property, rocks coming up out of the dirt
in the colors of: red's, yellow's and gray's
oh so very pretty, holes and fossils imprinted
in them made by the harsh weather over long
periods of time
it's all so very interesting to see, one could
get lost in the woods exploring, just enjoying
what nature has created here on earth the
beauty in it one could not describe in words alone
to paint what you see in front of you
would express more than my mere words could ever do
enjoy from what nature has provided for you
to explore what nature has created for us
it is truly a loss for all who do not see this

written: Aug. 10, 2006

One Moment

One moment that's all it takes
to change your life forever
in a blink of an eye everything
has changed for you in life
kinda like love at first sight
your not looking for that person
who is your other half of you
but their they are standing there
and everything you thought you
wanted in life, no longer
seems important to you
all you know is you want to spend
the rest of your life with them
to make all their dreams come true
one moment that's all it takes
to change your life forever
just one tiny moment that's it
your life has been changed
in the blink of an eye

written: Aug. 14, 2006

Feelings

Did you ever feel so confused
that you don't know if your coming or going
or what you should be feeling
at times I'm so happy
I wonder do I deserve this
this time in my life
but if I don't deserve this
what do I deserve from what life has to offer
I'm tired of feeling so confused
not sure where to turn to next
it's as if my life is still running me
instead of me controlling it
where do I stop the merry-go-round
to get off this spinning world I'm in
to finally put my mind at ease
so it can feel at peace
once and for all

written: Aug.20, 2006

Stop Living In The Past

We have to stop living in the past
we have to move on in life
look at all we're missing by livin' in the past
yes, I know it's not easy to do
but we deserve more from life
we have to stop letting people push us
around and take control of our lives now
your the only one who can do it
no—one else can do it for you
stop livin' in the past and move on with your life
it's your choice in life
you can be happy or you can continue to be sad
and so very lonely by yourself
what choice will you make

written: Nov. 19, 2006

A True Dreamer

I'm a true dreamer thru & thru
I hoped that one day I'd find
a love so pure it would
blow my mind to pieces
I've held to that dream for so long
I should of known better to
hope that I'd find Mr. Right
to dream that my Mr. Right
was out there searching for me
when will I ever learn
dreams are just that dreams

written: May 17, 2007

Just a look into the life of Kat Bussell:

Blonde Hair
Blue Eyes
5'3
A Hopeless Romantic
Loves Orange Roses

Enjoyments:
watching Romantic, Action & Comedy Movies
reading Romance Novels
writing Poems
Dreaming of the day
when I will find my Prince

Til then I will continue to write, dream
and wish upon a star
for my happy ever after

Kat

Thanks for buying my books!!!